It's Okay to Not Be Okay

AN INTERACTIVE JOURNAL
TO HELP YOU NAVIGATE THE HARD DAYS

DEAR FELLOW STRUGGLE BUS PASSENGER,

Welcome aboard!

As the artists behind *The Struggle Bus* Collection, we (Amber and Katie) wanted to create resources to help you through difficult times. When you find yourself in a valley, we want nothing more than to be right beside you, holding your hand, and letting you know that it's okay to feel the way you do. Through these pages, it is our hope that you know you're not alone. We are right beside you—listening, affirming, and supporting you.

We are by no means mental health experts, but we have found the practices and prompts within this journal helpful in our own lives and hope you find them so too. We've had our own heartaches and struggles (that are, of course, different than yours). We know that life is hard and messy. We will not sugarcoat that here.

Each seat on the struggle bus is equipped with a box of tissues because you are safe to cry the ugly tears here. We want this journal to be a companion that sits with you in the darkness—not rushing to turn on the light. Our hope is that you find comfort, connection, and reassurance that you are not alone.

It's okay to not be okay,

AMBER AND KATIE
Creators of *The Struggle Bus* Collection

To learn more about *The Struggle Bus* collection, go to dayspring.com/the-struggle-bus.

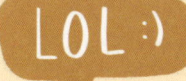

THIS JOURNAL BELONGS TO

_____

Contents

Sleepless Nights 6
Overcoming Comparison 14
Numbers 20
Movement 26
Poetry 32
Online & Offline 38
Faith & Doubt 44
When You Miss Someone 50
When Grief is No Stranger 58
Let's Make Some Playlists 66
For When You Feel Angry 72
It's the Little Things 80
Laughter & Stress 86
Burn Out 92
The Importance of Play 98
On Losing Motivation 104
Let's Talk Hope and Dreams 110
For When You Feel Scared 116
For When You Feel Guilt 124
For When You Worry 130
Let's Color 136
Failure, Grit & Praise 142
The Big Sad 148
For When You Feel Lonely 156
When You Don't Feel Like Cooking 162
Save This One For a Bad Day 170
Growing Pains 178
Miracle 184

Sleepless Nights

*So don't worry about tomorrow,
for tomorrow will bring its own worries.
Today's trouble is enough for today.*

MATTHEW 6:34 NIV

Ah, Night. That time of the day to lay our hard-worked body and mind to rest. But we toss and turn, and rest, it seems, is not interested in our company. It's like the more we think about how we need to sleep, the more awake we are. It's okay. Consider this chapter a companion who wants you to get rest but isn't rushing it.

WHERE DO YOU FEEL RESTLESS?

In the drawing below, color where you feel restless in red. Now color where you feel relaxed in blue. Stretch the restless red part of your body. Color over the red with blue. Your restless areas may not look perfectly blue, but they hopefully feel more relaxed and look a little less red.

GET IT OUT

Write a list of what's on your mind in this chest. Pretend that once you write it down it's locked. Give it to God. No more thinking about it . . . for tonight at least.

TRACING TIME

Let's trace some sleepy animals. Feel free to give them funny hats and mustaches.

EMBRACE THE NIGHT

Sometimes our bodies just aren't ready for sleep and that's okay. If we have to be awake, why not enjoy the night? Let's do some things that help us relax. Maybe it's taking a bath, doing some simple stretches, talking to God, or making a cup of tea.

What are some of your favorite things to think about?

What are some things that relax you?

THE PERFECT PLACE TO SLEEP

Sometimes it helps to visualize ourselves falling asleep. Let's dream up a peaceful place to doze off. Maybe it's a seaside or a cozy cabin in the woods. What would your perfect place to sleep be like?

What do you see?
_____
_____
_____

What do you smell?
_____
_____
_____

What do you hear?
_____
_____
_____

What do you feel?
_____
_____
_____

Write a small story about your perfect place to sleep. Try to include the things you listed above:
_____
_____
_____
_____
_____
_____

BE KIND TO YOURSELF.

Imagine adult you is with younger you. If little you was having a hard time falling asleep, how would adult you reassure little you? If adult you couldn't sleep, how would little you comfort adult you? Using kind words and gestures toward ourselves can help us when we feel frustrated. Write your thoughts in the bubbles to the right.

CHILD

How would big you comfort little you?

ADULT

How would little you comfort big you?

Overcoming Comparison

I praise you, for I am fearfully and wonderfully made. Wonderful are your works; my soul knows it very well

PSALM 139:14 ESV

Comparison—that thief of joy. What a jerk. If we are not careful, comparison can:

- turn into envy
- keep us from being fully present
- disconnect us from our community
- keep us from trusting our own voice and identity

How do we even begin to combat comparison? Let's explore some practices in this chapter to see if one of them helps.

COMPARISON MODE

There's a reason comparison steals our joy, and it's because we generally only see the highlight reel (on social media) or the surface level of what's actually going on with the other person. We think we've missed out on some secret that everyone else knows that we've somehow missed, and we can begin to doubt ourselves.

What are some areas in which you find yourself in comparison mode? Check them below

- ☐ Looks
- ☐ Kids
- ☐ Food
- ☐ Vacations
- ☐ Spouse
- ☐ Job
- ☐ Houses
- ☐ Weight
- ☐ Other: _____
- ☐ Cars
- ☐ Spending

CHOOSING THE BETTER ONE

Sometimes we think we must make *the* right choice—that there is one and only one right choice—and we must make a list of pros and cons and compare and contrast and decide once and for all and never change our minds till the end of time.

But there are times when comparing two good-yet-different things won't lead us to a definitive answer because they are *both* good and they could *both* lead to *good* outcomes. And each has things the other lacks.

For instance, take a look at the list below. Which is better? Can you decide? (Hint: you don't have to!)

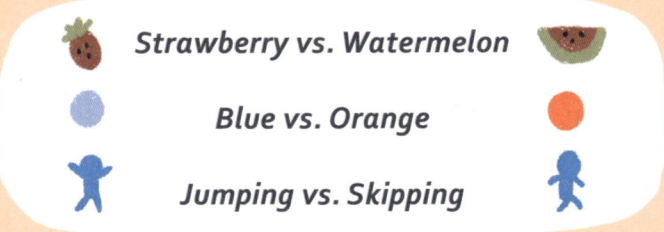

Now, try to think of a real-world example in your own life of something you compare. Are there good things about both? Could each produce a good outcome?

_____
_____
_____
_____
_____
_____
_____

GRATITUDE

It's easy to start comparing ourselves to others, especially when we feel as if others have it better than we do. One way we've found to stop the jealousy train is to play a mental slideshow of the people, places, and things we are thankful for in life. Write or sketch out your mental slideshow below.

QUIET THE INNER CRITIC

What does your inner critic say to you?

If you heard your friend saying that out loud, what would you say to them? How would you encourage them?

Now, say that to yourself.

FREEDOM

Here's the thing—if what works now doesn't work six months from now, we can change our minds! It's okay. We can move through our days free of worry that we missed our one and only chance to get it right.

Journal about some decisions you might like to revisit. How does it feel to realize that you *can* revisit them and change your mind? It can be something seemingly small like changing what you decided to wear for work or something that feels daunting like deciding to find a different preschool for your toddler because where they are isn't a good fit.

Numbers

The Word gave life to everything that was created, and his life brought light to everyone.
JOHN 1:4 NLT

Numbers. Why do we care so much about *numbers*? The number of years we've lived, the number of friends we have, the number on our jeans' tag, dollars in the bank, kids we have, rooms in our house . . . the list can go on and on. Numbers are an inherently neutral thing, and yet we assign value to them as if a number itself can bring us happiness and worth.

The numbers game is so exhausting.

We may have heard the message from our culture that "if you would just change *x*, *y*, and *z* about yourself, you would be happy."

But what we don't hear very often is that there is a lot that is *already* good about you—about all of us.

REMINDERS

Ask your friends and family what they like best about you.

Copy their responses here and/or write them on sticky notes. Place them where you can see them every day. Let these be your little pep talks each day. If you need to refresh them, reach out to your friends or family again.

you are the best COOK!

you are very kind

_____   _____
_____   _____
_____   _____
_____   _____
_____   _____
_____   _____
_____   _____
_____   _____
_____   _____
_____   _____
_____   _____
_____   _____

Write all the things you dislike about yourself in this box

Write all the things you like about yourself in this box

LET'S DO ONE OF THOSE BFF FILL-IN-THE-BLANK SHEETS.

I have been alive for _____ years.
THAT'S AMAZING!

I have/want a total of ____
(circle all that apply)
dogs, cats, pigs, cows, birds, bunnies,
(insert other animals here)
_____.
PETS ARE THE BEST! . . . UNLESS YOU'RE NOT A PET PERSON. THEN ZERO PETS FOR THE WIN!

My longest friendship has lasted _____ years.
FRIENDSHIP IS ONE OF THE BEST GIFTS!

My favorite book has _____ pages.
LOOK AT YOU READING AND LEARNING AND GROWING.

The number on my favorite pair of jeans is _____.

THIS NUMBER DOES NOT DEFINE YOUR WORTH.

What good associations do you have with the number you wrote above? Maybe you loved your 12th birthday party or perhaps your parents' anniversary is on November 28th.

List 2-3 here: _____

_____

My birthday is _____ / _____ / _____.

HAPPY BIRTHDAY TO YOU! YOU WEAR THOSE YEARS SO WELL.

My anniversary for _____
is _____ / _____ / _____.

HAPPIEST OF ANNIVERSARIES! WOO-HOO! LET'S CELEBRATE!

I have a total of _____ songs on my favorites playlist.

LET'S DANCE IT OUT!

Movement

*He makes the whole body fit together perfectly.
As each part does its own special work, it helps the other parts
grow, so that the whole body is healthy
and growing and full of love.*
EPHESIANS 4:16 NLT

Many of us have equated exercise with a sweaty, can't-catch-your-breath-or-you're-doing-it-wrong regimen. Or perhaps a sitting-on-the-couch-feeling-guilty-about-not-exercising routine. But what if we shifted our perspective? It's true that our bodies need to *move* to stay healthy. But *simple movement* can equal exercise, and movement can be *joyful*.

JOYFUL MOVEMENT

Our brains can literally get stuck in a rut, but our bodies can teach it *new* ways of being. Over the next few pages, let's try out some joyful movement ideas, just to get you started.

DANCE PARTY

Throw yourself a dance party. Turn on your favorite music and let your body *feel* it. Move accordingly. Notice what comes up for you.

How did you feel?
_____
_____

Were you able to let loose?
_____
_____

Try a different genre of music. Was anything different?
_____
_____

What happens if you invite others? Kids, spouse, friends?
_____
_____

WALK

Go on a walk outside. Or, if that's not possible for you, walk around your space. Let your senses take over.

What do you see? What do you smell?
_____
_____

What do you hear? What can you taste?
_____
_____

What can you touch along the way? How does it feel?
_____
_____

What can you listen to while walking that brings you joy?
Some ideas: a fun travel podcast, your favorite music, the next chapter in your audio book

_____
_____
_____
_____
_____
_____
_____

STRETCH

Take your shoes off and do some stretches.
    Notice your breath. Sit still and simply breathe. Count to three while you inhale. Count to four while you exhale. Notice where you are tense in your body. See if you can relax that part. Repeat.

How does your body feel?
_____
_____

What part of your body could use a stretch? Gently stretch it.
_____
_____

How does it feel to stretch sore muscles?
_____
_____

How does it feel to pay attention to your body and listen to what it needs?
_____
_____
_____
_____

What movement do you find joyful? Why?

If you're having trouble grasping the concept of "joyful" movement, what's holding you back from shifting to a joyful perspective of movement? What step could you take (maybe a literal, physical step) to make the shift?

_____
_____
_____
_____

Poetry

*They are like trees planted by streams of water,
which yield their fruit in its season,
and their leaves do not wither.
In all that they do, they prosper.*

PSALM 1:3 NRSV

Poems can help us express our deepest feelings in a new, beautiful way. They can help us understand or process how we might feel about the stuff we're going through or help us vent about the unfair things that happen to us. We're going to make specific poems that express our own feelings. We suggest you come back to this chapter and fill out whichever poem prompt speaks to you on any specific day. Or feel free to fill out this entire chapter at once. You can approach this chapter any way you'd like to. We just want you to have fun with it!

Write a poem to your future self.

Write a poem about a bittersweet memory.

Write a poem to an alien about being human.

Write a poem about one of your most vivid, beautiful memories.

Write a poem to a stranger. Leave it somewhere.

Online & Offline

And let us consider how to stir up one another to love and good works, not neglecting to meet together, as is the habit of some, but encouraging one another, and all the more as you see the Day drawing near.

HEBREWS 10:24–25 ESV

Let's face it, social media comes with a lot of curveballs. One minute you're scrolling through happy photos of friends and family, and the next minute you're being subjected to negativity at the highest level. Online social sites can bring feelings of joy and hope, or they can bring feelings of disappointment and even anger. That's why it's important to think through how we use these powerful tools.

REACT BUTTONS

Draw your most-used social apps below and take note of the emotions that come up when you're using them. Take note of how you feel after you've put your phone down.

During
After

During
After

During
After

During
After

During
After

During
After

WATCH YOUR WATCH

Many social apps are designed to keep us engaged. While spending time on our apps can be fun, it's easy to lose track of time and spend more minutes on our phones than we'd like.

How many hours do you spend on your phone each day?

Keep track of how many times you check your phone over the next couple of days:

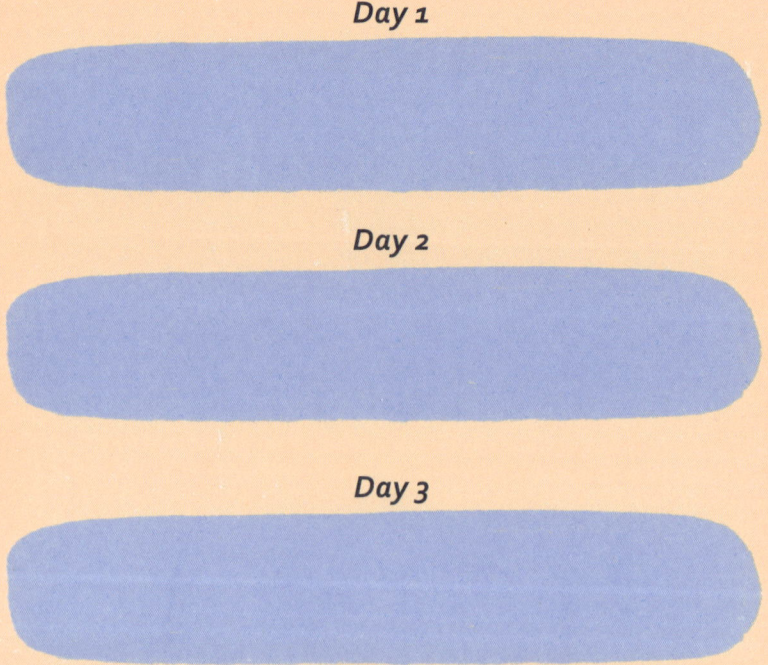

How do you feel about your social media usage?

Is there something you would rather be doing with this time?

ONLINE YOU VERSUS OFFLINE YOU

Think about who you are online and who you are offline.

What are some differences between the two?

Write them in the spaces down below.

ONLINE

OFFLINE

WHO DO YOU WANT TO BE?

Who do you want to be offline?
___
___
___
___
___

Who do you want to be online?
___
___
___
___
___

What are some first steps that you can make?
___
___
___
___
___

When do you feel the most like yourself?
___
___
___
___
___

Faith & Doubt

Faith shows the reality of what we hope for; it is the evidence of things we cannot see.
HEBREWS 11:1 NLT

Doubting our faith can sometimes feel like a darkened cave, full of twisting paths, dead ends, and shadows, and if we enter, we are afraid we may not find our way out to the light again.

In the Bible, the writer of the book of Hebrews says that "faith shows the reality of what we hope for; it is the evidence of things we cannot see" (11:1 NLT). Exploring doubt can allow us to know, in a deeper way, what that truly means.

It's like shining a light into the cave and noticing there are tunnels leading off in all directions. Exploring leads us to places we might not be able to fathom a way out of, but because we have already traveled so far, we can have hope that our steps of faith will lead us through.

At first glance, it seems nonsensical. But experiencing doubt allows us to experience *faith* and *hope*. The faith and hope may look different than expected, but *they are also deeper and wider than seemingly possible.*

EXPLORATION

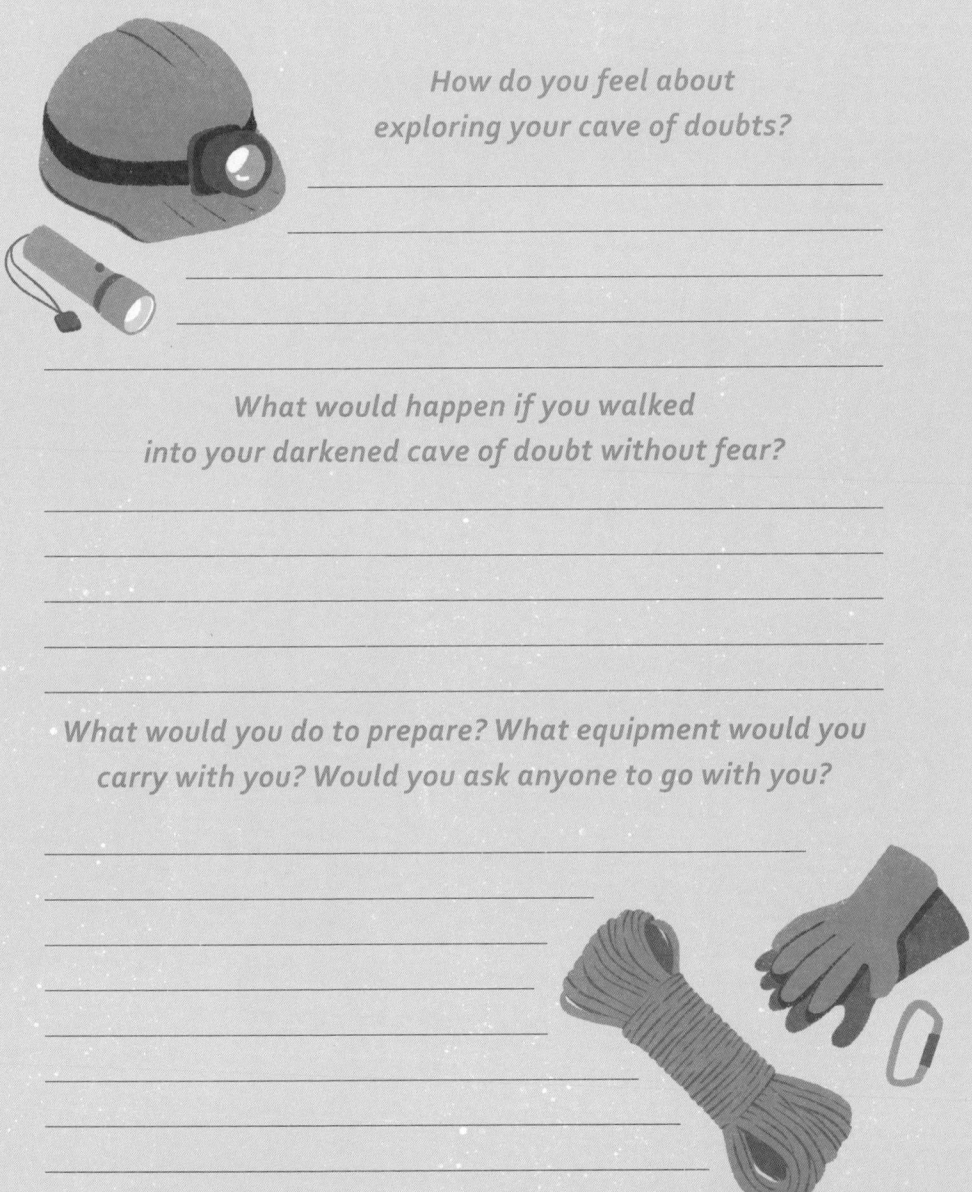

How do you feel about exploring your cave of doubts?

_____
_____
_____
_____

What would happen if you walked into your darkened cave of doubt without fear?

_____
_____
_____
_____
_____

What would you do to prepare? What equipment would you carry with you? Would you ask anyone to go with you?

_____
_____
_____
_____
_____
_____
_____

QUESTIONS & ANSWERS

What are the questions you are afraid to ask?

What answers would you seek?

What would it look like to invite Christ into those doubts?
Not to resolve them but to sit with Him
amid those doubts as an act of faith.

DOUBTS

Doubt allows us to ask questions, seek discernment, and find out that the answers are not always black and white. Sometimes there is not an easy answer, or there is no answer at all.

Try writing your doubts in the middle of this cavern. Leave them there for a while (an hour? a day? a year? Whatever is needed).

SHINE A LIGHT

Occasionally, we find ourselves at a dead end and don't know where to turn.

What steps of faith can you take to shine a light on those doubts?

Some ideas that might help get you started:
- Talk with a trusted mentor.
- Practice focusing on the awe and wonder of faith versus the certainty of answers.
- Trust that your steps of faith will be enough to see you through.

FAITH & HOPE

Have you experienced doubt turning into the gems of deeper faith and hope in your own life? In what way(s)?

When You Miss Someone

Blessed are those who mourn.
MATTHEW 5:4 NIV

There's no easy introduction to this chapter. If only grief were something we didn't have to experience. Trying to find the words to say to someone on this subject is a daunting endeavor to say the least. Grief is such a heaviness that we all experience and process differently. Just know this: It's okay to not be okay. It's okay to take the time you need. It's okay to cry in unexpected places, at unexpected things.

This chapter is dedicated to:

_____

From:

_____

CRY

That's all we can do sometimes.

WRITE THEM A LETTER

What would you say to them now?
What's something you wish you could have said?
What's something you want them to know?

BONFIRE NIGHT

On a separate piece of paper, write a list of all your regrets. The things that you wish you would have done, or didn't do, things said or unsaid, and so on. Once you've written them all down, build a small bonfire. (You can go camping if you don't have access to a firepit). Rip up that paper of regrets, bit by bit, and throw it in the fire when the flames get going strong.

If you'd like, feel free to ask your friends or family members to join you. Perhaps they are grieving along with you, or maybe they are grieving for someone else. You can all benefit from being together around the fire.

CREATE A MEMORIAL

This could be a work of art, a small piece of jewelry with their picture, or even a playlist of songs that you both enjoyed—whatever helps you to express your feelings and pay tribute to the person you are grieving. Journal about what you did here.

WRITE THEM A POEM

LEGACY LIVES ON

Do something in memory of them. If your grandpa liked roses, plant some roses; if your friend liked to cook, give her favorite recipes a go.

Journal about your experience here.

WHAT WOULD THEY SAY?

What do you think this person would say if they were here? How would they want you to live without them?

_____
_____
_____
_____
_____
_____
_____
_____
_____
_____
_____
_____
_____
_____
_____
_____
_____
_____
_____
_____
_____
_____
_____
_____

When Grief is No Stranger

Come to Me, all you who are weary and burdened, and I will give you rest.
MATTHEW 11:28 NIV

If we have lived very long at all, grief is no stranger to us.

In this chapter, we'd like to explore grief in contexts outside of the loss of a person (see the "When You Miss Someone" chapter if that applies to you).

Grief can encompass a whole range of losses. And probably the best thing to do when we experience loss is to truly experience it. Notice the loss. Let it be present. Allow our bodies to feel all our feelings. Only then can we hope to make it through to the other side—whatever that may look like for each of us.

Please be gentle with yourself and take this chapter as slowly as you need to. If you find these feelings are too difficult to face right now, feel free to simply leave it blank!

MOVING

Moving can be exciting—experiencing new places, new people, new routines. But moving can also feel like a loss—a lost sense of place, of purpose, of "normal."

When have you moved?
_____
_____
_____

What loss did you experience?
_____
_____
_____

What did you leave behind?
_____
_____
_____

What feelings come up for you when you think about that experience?
_____
_____
_____

CHILDHOOD

This may feel like a weird one because growing up is such an integral part of life. But it's okay to grieve the loss of your childhood—of your innocence and lack of responsibility. Some of us lose our childhood earlier than we should for a whole host of reasons.

What did it feel like when you realized you were no longer in childhood?

_____
_____
_____

What loss did you experience?

_____
_____
_____

What did you leave behind?

_____
_____
_____

What feelings come up for you when you think about that experience?

_____
_____
_____

HEALTH

Our health is so easy to take for granted—until it is no longer there. Whether it's an accident, a lifestyle choice, an injury, an illness, or a disease, health can slip from our grasp or be taken away in an instant.

When have you experienced health loss?

_____
_____
_____
_____

What did you leave behind?

_____
_____
_____
_____

What feelings come up for you when you think about that experience?

_____
_____
_____
_____

COLLECTIVE GRIEF

The Covid-19 global pandemic brought a collective grief along with it. In the year 2020, it seemed as if no one was untouched by the effects of the pandemic.

What comes to mind when you think about the global pandemic?

_____
_____
_____

What loss did you experience?

_____
_____
_____

What feelings come up for you when you think about your experience?

_____
_____
_____
_____

JOB

When we lose a job (even if it was our choice but especially if it wasn't), we can lose not just our source of income but our feelings of security, self-worth, and confidence.

When have you experienced job loss?

_____
_____
_____
_____
_____
_____
_____

What feelings come up for you when you think about that experience?

_____
_____
_____
_____
_____
_____
_____

FRIENDS / RELATIONSHIPS

Losing a friend or any significant relationship in our life can feel like losing part of ourselves. It's an especially hard loss because while that person may not have died, our relationship with them did. And whether the relationship died a slow, tortuous death or a quick, painful one, it can leave scars.

When have you experienced the loss of a friend or relationship?

_____
_____
_____

What feelings come up for you when you think about that experience?

_____
_____
_____
_____
_____
_____
_____

COMMUNITY

There are lots of reasons why we can lose a community through the normal ebbs and flows of life. We can lose community for all the reasons in this chapter: when we move, lose our childhood, lose our health, experience a pandemic, change jobs, lose a friend or relationship. Other reasons might include changing churches, entering into a new life stage, and so on.

When have you experienced the loss of community?

_____
_____
_____
_____

What feelings come up for you when you think about that experience?

_____
_____
_____
_____

Let's Make Some Playlists

"But get me a musician."
And then, while the musician was playing,
the power of the LORD came on him.
II KINGS 3:15 NRSV

What songs bring you comfort? What songs make you feel happy? Music can express our emotions, hold our most special of memories, and help us feel understood. It's likely that there's a song out there that feels like it was written just for you. We want to take some time and give you a space to research and explore.

SONGS AND MOOD

We know there are a lot of these. We wanted to make it specific. If you don't listen to music when you feel a mood that is listed below, try to best guess what you might listen to if you were to feel this way.

What songs would you listen to if you felt . . .

Sad:

Angry:

Happy:

Thankful:

Excited:

Tired:

Loved:

Hurt:

Relieved:

Peaceful:

Hopeful:

Content:

Nostalgic:

Alive:

Strong:

WHAT SOUNDS DESCRIBE YOU?

If you had to make a playlist for the past five years of your life, what songs would go on it? What songs would symbolize your growth, hardships, and experiences? Write them below.

- ★
- ★
- ★
- ★
- ★
- ★
- ★
- ★
- ★
- ★
- ★
- ★

DESIGN YOUR COVER

Every great album or track has great art to accompany it. Draw, or use photos, stickers, stamps—whatever is available to you—to design your five-year playlist.

MUSIC FOR MEMORIES

*Make a playlist of the songs
that hold your favorite memories.*

SONG	MEMORY

Make another playlist of songs you'd like to make memories to.

TRADE PLAYLISTS

Ask a friend or family member to make a list of ten to fifteen songs that they think best describe you. Do the same for them and swap playlists.

Write them both down here:

my playlist for:

-
-
-
-
-
-
-
-
-
-
-
-
-
-
-

A playlist for me made by:

-
-
-
-
-
-
-
-
-
-
-
-
-
-
-

For When You Feel Angry

*If the anger of the ruler rises against you,
do not leave your place,
for calmness will lay great offenses to rest.*
ECCLESIASTES 10:4 ESV

Hey there. If you're here because you're upset, we're sorry that today hasn't gone well. Life can be cruddy like that sometimes. Know that getting angry is okay. It's human. Journaling out that stuff can be helpful, so we're happy you're here. Let's get started.

THE VOLCANO

If 10 is anger eruption, where are you on the scale right now?

Color in your level within the volcano. Flex your muscles for however long your anger level might be. (Flex for 6 seconds if you colored a 6 in the scale.) Start with your arms, then legs, fingers, and finally toes. Remember to breathe. Focus on how they feel on the release. Relax your shoulders. Unclench your jaw.

HOW TO GET MAD

Let's play devil's advocate. Make a list of ways to get angry. This could be not getting enough sleep, skipping meals, eating food that makes you feel sluggish, spending too much time online, expecting perfection from yourself, and so on.

GRRRR

Are there things on this list that might be adding to your frustrations?

Would changing some of them help? How so?

DISRUPTING THE ERUPTION

When we get mad, it helps us to do something to disrupt or challenge that feeling and bring down our angry meter. This could look like taking a walk, talking to God, doing some jumping jacks, or spending time with a pet.

What helps cool you down?

_____
_____
_____
_____
_____
_____
_____
_____
_____
_____
_____
_____
_____
_____
_____
_____
_____

EXPRESS YOURSELF

Draw or write out your feelings here.

DEAR ANGER

Write a letter to your anger.

It's The Little Things

Finally, brothers, whatever is true, whatever is honorable, whatever is just, whatever is pure, whatever is lovely, whatever is commendable, if there is any excellence, if there is anything worthy of praise, think about these things.

PHILIPPIANS 4:8 ESV

With the busy lives we live, it's easy to pass by some of life's more quiet and humble details. Sometimes our focus is on future appointments or plans, and we can miss the beauty happening around us in the present. Being mindful of little details can enrich our days, help us appreciate all of God's beautiful creation, and help us feel more connected to the world around us.

STOP AND SMELL THE ROSES

It might be walking to school, driving to work, or even getting out of bed and walking to the bathroom. There is subtle beauty in the regular path we cross each day that we've probably overlooked.

Take the time to notice something new on one of these regular paths you take.

What did you notice?

_____
_____
_____
_____

What, if anything, has changed from when you first took this regular path?

_____
_____
_____
_____

In what other places could you be mindful of the details?

_____
_____
_____
_____

TRACE YOUR HAND HERE

Draw in all the little details. (Beautiful!)

LET'S TAKE SOME PICTURES...!

... but don't travel anywhere. Actually, from where you are right now, try to find interesting colors or perspectives to take photos of. Sit on the floor, pull out your phone or camera, move things around, and play around with the lighting.

What did you find?

_____
_____
_____
_____
_____
_____
_____
_____

What's your favorite photo and why?

_____
_____
_____
_____
_____
_____
_____
_____

WATCH THE GRASS GROW

There's life happening all around us, even in the most overlooked places. Find an interesting patch of grass outside.

Record or sketch what you see, smell, feel:

Laughter & Stress

And Sarah declared, "God has brought me laughter. All who hear about this will laugh with me."
GENESIS 21:6 NLT

LOL :)

This might seem a bit counterintuitive at first, but there are loads of benefits to cracking a joke or two at the wrong time. Laughter releases endorphins, helps relax our bodies, boosts our immune system, and lowers our stress hormones. Having a laugh can be a powerful and effective way to handle absurd and zany situations.

WHEN YOU NEED A LAUGH

What's your all-time favorite joke?

What's made you laugh recently?

What are some go-to comedy movies/podcasts you enjoy?

When is the last time you made someone laugh?

COMICS AND CONNECTION

Comics often take normal, mundane events and view them in a comedic perspective. The same can be said for unfortunate situations. Let's draw out one of our recent frustrations.

ROSES ARE RED, VIOLETS ARE BLUE . . .

. . . this prompt is about nasty old fondue! Just kidding, not really. That'd be gross. But we *are* going to do some silly writing! Let's make some funny short poems. These can be about work, responsibilities, whatever stress feels fun to poke at.

Here's our example—we like to make it rhyme:

Writing a book is fun, but we are ready to be done.
We'd think you'd laugh, if you saw our first draft.
Writing these pages has been no joke,
But it's all worth it for you friendly folks.

Now you try!

THE PERFECT WORKPLACE

Let's dream up a perfect workplace! Without looking at the text on the next page, fill out the blank spaces below with what is prompted. Then write them in the story on the next page.

(adjective) _____

(adjective) _____

(article of clothing, plural) _____

(adjective) _____

(noun) _____

(exclamation) _____

(geographical location) _____

(adjective) _____

(land formation) _____

(number) _____

(style of attire) _____

THE PERFECT WORKPLACE

A great workplace must have people who are _____
(adjective)

and wear _____ _____.
(adjective) (article of clothing, plural)

Their coworkers would feel _____ in this
(adjective)

environment. There would be free _____ in the
(noun)

break room, and when people pass you in the hallway,

they would say, "_____!"
(exclamation)

The company would be located in _____
(geographical location)

and right next to a/an _____ _____!
(adjective) (land formation)

The only requirements are that you take a mandatory

_____-week vacation every year and dress
(number)

_____ every Friday. These are the things
(style of attire)

that would make up a perfect workplace!

Burn Out

*He said to them, "Come away to a deserted place
all by yourselves and rest a while."
For many were coming and going,
and they had no leisure even to eat.*

MARK 6:31 NRSV

Burnout is a special type of tired. It's when you've worked your hardest to get something done and responsibilities just keep coming. It can feel like there's no room to even celebrate the little things we've accomplished. Please know you're not alone in feeling this. Feeling burned out won't last forever, and hopefully we can give you a few ideas to help deal with it.

SHAKE IT OUT

Get up and shake your body. Shake out the frustration, the stress, and the overwhelming tasks. Jump and stomp and loosen it up. Stretch your limbs. Take deep breaths.

THE PRESSURE COOKER

Let's pretend your stress is hot steam and you are the pressure cooker. You've got to release some of that hot steam; otherwise you risk building up too much pressure. In the drawing, jot a list of stressors that add to your pressure buildup.

What does releasing some of that stress steam look like for you?

It could be asking for some help, scheduling time away, or getting in some time at the gym. Write down some of your bigger stresses and try to be specific about how to handle those.

PRIORITIZE SOME MINI-VACATION TIME

What's a mini-vacation, you ask? It could be taking a trip to the animal shelter to hold some puppies, eating your lunch in the park, or just feeling the grass between your toes. These are sneaky ways to fit in feel-good, relaxing things into your busy schedule.

List some mini-vacations you'd like to take soon:

What are some you can take today? Right now?

CELEBRATE THE LITTLE WINS

Even if it's as little as finishing this chapter, the little things deserve to be celebrated. These could be putting on some shoes, sorting the laundry, or even making a list of what you'd like to do.

What are some little things you've accomplished today?

The Importance of Play

I have come that they may have life and have it to the full.
JOHN 10:10 NIV

When we grow up, we can forget how important giving ourselves time to play is. Being playful and lighthearted as adults can feel just as good as it did when we were little. It can help release stress, help us laugh off some of our hardest days, and help us enjoy the abundance that life has to offer.

WHAT A WONDERFUL WORLD

What brought you wonder as a kid? Stars? Dinosaurs? Snowfall?

_____
_____
_____
_____
_____
_____
_____
_____
_____

What brings you wonder now?

_____
_____
_____
_____
_____
_____
_____
_____

FINDING BALANCE

Taking time out of our schedules to enjoy things can be difficult. Sometimes our responsibilities demand most of our time. We can forget how important it is to have fun and to enjoy the life God has given us.

*What looks like a good balance for you?
Write down your responsibilities and the things you do
for fun. Pretend the scale moves with weight,
which means no overloading the obligations!*

Responsibilities

Fun Things

YOUNG AT HEART

What makes you feel young again?

When was the last time you did something on this list?

What's stopped you from having more fun?

NO SHAME IN NOSTALGIA

Take yourself on a bike ride, a neighborhood walk, or an evening drive. Listen to your favorite music from when you were younger.

Make your playlist here:

NO TIME LIKE THE PRESENT

If you were face-to-face with a younger you, what would younger you want you to remember as an adult?

_____
_____
_____
_____
_____
_____
_____
_____

What do you want your future self to remember ten, fifteen, or twenty years from now?

Write a note to yourself. Keep it somewhere you will remember to open it later in life, or stow it in this journal for safekeeping!

_____
_____
_____
_____
_____
_____
_____
_____

On Losing Motivation

Let us not become weary in doing good, for at the proper time we will reap a harvest if we do not give up.
GALATIANS 6:9 NIV

Building and maintaining motivation for moving toward a goal can be like running a marathon. The send-off is awesome, the breeze feels great, and there are all these people jogging beside you. Then some people drop out. Your muscles start to ache, and the path ahead seems emptier than before. What keeps you going? What makes you push through the mile markers?

BREATHE

Give yourself compassion. Running races and working toward goals are no easy feats. If motivation runs low, it may just be because it's tiring work. Try to learn when you are in a state of fatigue. This is your body's way of telling you it could use a break.

When you think about the goal you are working toward, is there any part of your body that feels tired? Where?

Do you give it breaks often?

PIT STOPS

What makes you feel rested?

What makes your body feel recharged?

What gives you energy?

FAN YOUR PASSION

Imagine your passion for this goal as a fire in a firepit. What would be the fuel for your fire? What would you throw in to keep it going? How would you maintain it? Write these things below.

ONE SMALL STEP

Even if it's wobbly walking toward your finish line, you are making progress. Each little step means progress, and each little step is worth celebrating. Draw an outline of your shoe here and write all the little steps you've made toward your goal. Even if it's just getting out of bed each morning.

Let's Talk Hope And Dreams

"'If you can'?" said Jesus.
"Everything is possible for one who believes."
MARK 9:23 NIV

Hopes and dreams don't always have to be centered around a career. We can hope to be closer to our friends in the future or dream that we will become stronger and wiser individuals. For this chapter we want to give you a space to dream big, in any way you see fit. Try to answer these questions from a few different perspectives. Maybe you will learn something new about yourself!

I hope that one day I will . . .

My dream is to be . . .

I hope that I can be _____ when I am older.

Hopes and dreams I have accomplished are . . .

I've carried this dream for a long time . . .

A hope I've committed to is . . .

A dream or hope that was given to me by another individual is . . .

**When you leave this world,
what good things do you hope you'll leave behind?**

**My hopes and dreams are important because
(fill out the entire space) . . .**

My dream for the people around me is . . .

A dream I had in the past that I still have today is . . .

A hope that has been fulfilled time and time again is . . .

For When You Feel Scared

*Do not be afraid, little flock,
for it is your Father's good pleasure
to give you the kingdom.*
LUKE 12:32 NRSV

There's a lot in the world to be to be afraid of. Snakes, spiders, two-week-old leftovers—you name it. Fear can help keep us safe from things like poisonous animals, but it can also keep us from doing something we want to do. Life can be scary. It's okay to feel scared. It's normal. Let's talk about it.

THE BIG ONE

What's your biggest fear?

POV (POINT OF VIEW)

Fears can affect how we see the world. Maybe people seem scary, or big goals look unachievable.

What do you see in your fear lenses?
What might look different if you could take them off?

ON

OFF

REMINISCING ON BRAVERY

Think of a time in your life when you were the bravest you've ever been.

What fear did you feel in that moment?
_____
_____
_____
_____
_____

What was it like afterward?
_____
_____
_____
_____
_____

Did it change you? How so?
_____
_____
_____
_____
_____
_____
_____

ILLUSTRATED FEAR

If your fear had a metaphorical face, what would it look like? Maybe it's a big monster with sharp teeth, or maybe it's a ball made of scribbles. Draw or describe it below.

TAKE CARE

If you could make a care package for your fear, what would it look like? Would snacks or a movie help your fear feel better? What would help your fear feel braver? Draw the items below.

CONSULT YOUR FEAR

Let's try to imagine we're interviewing your fear for an upcoming job—a job as in something you might be afraid of trying or nervous to do. Your fear is going to want to protect you, but how do you know if it's holding you back? Let's try to ask your fear some questions to see what we may learn about it.

Tell me about your fear.

What motivates your fear?

How does your fear deal with stressful situations?

What type of work environment does your fear prefer?

What is your fear's greatest personal achievement?

What's your fear most passionate about?

What makes your fear unique?

What are your fear's greatest strengths?

What are your fear's greatest weaknesses?

For When You Feel Guilt

*My grace is sufficient for you,
for my power is made perfect in weakness.*
II CORINTHIANS 12:9 NIV

Ugh, guillllllt. It can be so ubiquitous to our daily lives we don't know how to live without it. We feel guilty (I've done something bad) for all sorts of things which can very quickly tumble into a sense of shame (I am bad). Guilt can be useful, though. It helps us realize we've done something (or not done something) that hurt ourselves or someone else. Guilt, just like anger or sadness or joy, is an emotion. Emotions are neither good nor bad. They simply are how we are feeling at any given moment.

In this chapter, let's explore reasons we might feel guilty and ways to help overcome those feelings of guilt so that we do not get stuck.

PERFECTION

Ah, the trap of perfection. When we cannot seem to do everything "right" we can feel guilt. But let us remind ourselves: no one is perfect. No one is perfect. No one is perfect.

What are areas in your life where you feel this trap of perfection and guilt the most?

_____
_____
_____
_____
_____
_____
_____

Does it help to say to yourself: no one is perfect?

_____
_____
_____
_____
_____
_____
_____
_____
_____

SELF-COMPASSION

Guilt often stems from a mistake. One way we can overcome the feeling of guilt is to first accept what we are feeling. Agree that we messed up and tell ourselves we'll do better next time. Then, ask ourself how we can take care of ourself right there, in the moment.

What things come to mind with this practice?

NEXT TIME

When we get stuck feeling guilty, it can be hard to change our behavior. Sometimes it can take practice to get unstuck.

Instead of thinking "I should have..." we can pivot slightly to "Next time I want to..." That simple shift can help us practice being okay with not getting it right and help us feel empowered to do it differently.

What "shoulds" do you have that you can change into "next times"?

OTHER PEOPLE

When our actions cause pain for other people, what can we do? Sometimes, the simplest approach is the most powerful: apologize. Apologize specifically. Allow the other person to feel their feelings. We can be compassionate and responsive to them while knowing we are not responsible for how other people feel. Repeat: we are not responsible for how other people feel.

Are there any people whom you'd like to apologize to?

_____
_____
_____
_____
_____
_____

How would you go about that?

_____
_____
_____
_____
_____
_____
_____
_____
_____

HELP

Sometimes we experience guilt over things we have no control over. Maybe we survived when someone else didn't. Sometimes we still experience guilt from things that happened a long time ago. It's important to note that these feelings of guilt are normal, and you are not alone. That doesn't mean you feel any less stuck, though. It's possible to seek professional help for those feelings.

How does it feel to think about seeking out professional help? What are some steps you could take to get there?

For When You Worry

*Can all your worries
add a single moment to your life?*
MATTHEW 6:27 NLT

Worry cannot change the past. It cannot change the present. It cannot change the future. But when has that *ever* stopped us from spending copious amounts of our precious time worrying? When we worry, it's generally about things that are beyond our control.

ACCEPTANCE

What are some things you worry about that you cannot control? Can you accept that you can't control everything? Write out how that makes you feel here.

_____
_____
_____
_____
_____
_____
_____
_____
_____
_____
_____
_____
_____
_____
_____
_____
_____

PLAN AHEAD

When worry takes hold, it can be hard to imagine a positive outcome. In those instances, it can be helpful to have a plan of attack. If the worst-case scenario happens, what are some things you would do? Write them down. Having a plan can help ease our worries.

DISTRACTIONS

Worry can suck all the joy from our days. Doing something we enjoy can help break the cycle of negative thoughts. If only for a moment, it can give us a reprieve from the worry.

What are some things you really enjoy?

Does it help relieve your worry to take a break and do them?

BIG & SMALL

When we are filled with worries, we can forget about all the *good* things in our life too. The worry feels so BIG that everything else is small in comparison. Our world and our life are so much bigger than the things we worry about. Remembering the good things—even if they're small, even if it takes us a minute to find them—can help us handle our worries.

What are some small things you are grateful for today? Write them in the leaves below.

TIME IT

If worry is an all-day endeavor, we can try giving it a time limit. Allow yourself to write down all the worries you have but *only* for a limited time each day, like just ten minutes. Then put that paper away. If you find yourself worrying after those ten minutes, simply tell yourself you can think about those worries again tomorrow during their set time limit.

*If you try this, how did it go?
Write about your experience here.*

_____
_____
_____
_____
_____
_____
_____
_____
_____
_____
_____
_____
_____
_____
_____
_____
_____

Let's Color

As the light approaches,
the earth takes shape like clay pressed beneath a seal;
it is robed in brilliant colors.
JOB 38:14 NLT

This is simply a chapter to color. Nuthin' more, nuthin' less. Have fun!

SMALL HOPS MAKE FROGRESS

GO GET 'EM, TIGER!

OH WELL!

YOU LOOK GOOD OUT THERE,
DOING YOUR BEST EVERY DAY.

WE ARE CHEERING YOU ON EVERY DAY!

Failure, Grit & Praise

So encourage each other and build each other up, just as you are already doing.
I THESSALONIANS 5:11 NLT

Think about the best stories you've heard, the best movies you've watched, or the best books you've read. You know, the ones that keep you guessing with their twists and turns, heartaches and triumphs. What does a great story have? A happy ending? Not necessarily. An easy outcome? No way. Every good story includes disappointment, tragedy, or some failure that the character(s) must overcome. Failure isn't the end of the story. It's the turning point. The helpful (painful) prod in a different direction. Doing something scary, that might make you fail, at the least, will always (eventually) make for a great story.

GRIT & YET

Let's talk about grit. Grit is that quality we have when we are able to keep going even after we fail—when failure doesn't force us to a halt but forces us forward, determined to figure out a way through. Our self-talk may be the most important thing in finding that grit. Instead of "I can't figure this out" try "I haven't figured this out *yet*." That tiny little word "yet" can be the catalyst that pushes us forward instead of allowing failure to be the final word.

What self-talk can you add the word "yet" to?

_____
_____
_____
_____
_____
_____

How does that change its outlook for you?

_____
_____
_____
_____
_____
_____
_____
_____

NOTHING WASTED

All of our experiences can help us move forward. There is nothing we've done that is wasted. And since nothing is wasted, even the smallest amount of work or progress can help us meet our goals and overcome that fear of failure. Want to learn a new language? Even five, ten, fifteen minutes a day can help you get there.

Do you feel like something you've done has been wasted effort? How could you rephrase it or see it in a different light?

What are some small things you can do to help you meet your goals and overcome your fear of failure?

DON'T SHARE

Everyone has to start somewhere. In the age of social media, though, it can feel like we must share progress reports publicly. However, the fear of the public eye can cause us to quit before we even begin. But what if we DIDN'T share? What if we tried something new simply for the pleasure of learning something new? When we try things out and fail and get better and fail and change and learn and grow, we can practice "failing" in ways that feel safe. Then, when our boss or peer or doctor asks us to do something new, we'll have some memory muscles of whats it's like to fail and yet keep going.

Perhaps you want to learn how to keep a plant alive or make the perfect pie crust. What is something you've always wanted to try that you could fail at privately and yet keep going to try to get even a little bit better?

PRAISE #1

Think of a time in your life when you've failed something or someone. Can you applaud that failure? Try telling it "good job" and write out all the things that failure helped you learn.

_____
_____
_____
_____
_____
_____
_____
_____
_____
_____
_____
_____
_____
_____
_____
_____
_____
_____
_____
_____
_____
_____

PRAISE #2

This might seem counterintuitive for some of us, but *other people's success does not diminish or negate our own*. This world is sooo big, and the human capacity for creativity is second only to our Creator. And, fun fact, when we focus on encouraging and cheering others on, we cannot also focus on our own failings. Another fun thing about encouragement is that it almost always encourages the giver AND receiver.

Who can you encourage in their pursuits/relationships/all around awesomeness today?

Get out your phone and send them a text or email right now. Then come back and write out what you did. You'll be encouraged every time you see it!

The Big Sad

*For the enemy has pursued me,
crushing my life to the ground,
making me sit in darkness like those long dead.
Therefore my spirit faints within me;
my heart within me is appalled.*

PSALM 143:3–4 NRSV

Depression. It's a heavy word, but it's real. In some shape or form, it's most likely touched all of us. Like a lot of different subjects, people can experience this in many ways. Please know, there is absolutely no shame in it. Depression is not your fault. Being human is complicated and crazy hard with slumps we can't foresee or control. It can come with a lot of emotions, so try to give yourself a break. A lot of admirable people have been through or are going through this. Crying, stillness, the blueness of it all—it's just a part of life. It's a painful part of loving deeply and experiencing the world around us.

THE STUFF YOU DON'T WANT TO HEAR

Okay. So. First things first. Let's list all the stuff you really don't want to hear right now. There's a ton of advice around this subject, and not everything resonates with everyone. Let's make this guy right here the bad guy. Let's call him bad-advice-Kevin. Sorry if your name's Kevin... It's not personal. Promise.

What bad advice would bad-advice-Kevin give you?

THE STUFF YOU DO WANT TO HEAR

So ... now that we got all the stuff we don't resonate with out of the way ... What's some stuff that sounds appealing? If you were in a movie right now and the main character walks in the room and says exactly what you need to hear, what would it be? What would bring you some comfort or reassurance?

He's taking notes

COMFORT CHARACTERS

Sometimes when we're going through a hard time, having comfort characters to look to is helpful. Maybe these characters are from books, movies, tv shows, or even your life, who make you feel a little bit better. What's comforting about them? Are there things that they say that you like?

Make a small list of your favorites here. Feel free to include quotes or characteristics you like from them.

CHARACTER	CHARACTERISTICS

FINDING CONNECTION IN THE ARTS

Forms of human expression come in many different avenues. There are movies, music, literature, poetry, paintings, and the list goes on. When we think about the emotions we may be going through right now, the words can sometimes be hard to find. Chances are there are quite a few people who have been through something similar. Among those are probably some people who have written poetry or made paintings about it.

Art can offer us some connection. Although we're usually total strangers, hearing a song or seeing a painting that represents our shared emotions can help us feel a little less alone in it.

When you think of works of art that you find comforting, what comes to mind? Are there specific songs or imagery that you think of?

_____
_____
_____
_____

Try searching for a new piece of art. This can come in any form you like, such as music, poetry, etc. What do you like about it? Does it represent your feelings in a way you resonate with, and if so, how so?

_____
_____
_____
_____
_____

Is there a work of art that makes you feel hopeful? Describe that work of art and why it makes you feel hopeful.

TAKE THE PRESSURE OFF

Write down all your responsibilities, insecurities, worries, stressors, or anything you find to be burdensome on the jacket below. Try to only think about it long enough to get it written down.

Allow yourself a moment to exist outside of those responsibilities and worries.

When we look back at that list, we get to choose which things we want to 'put on' / tackle. Keep in mind your energy level and what is achievable now. Try to dress appropriately, as to not put on seven different shirts (aka responsibilities or worries) at once.

What are some things you feel comfortable wearing and or dealing with today?

If the answer is none or even just one thing—that is more than okay. There is always tomorrow.

For When You Feel Lonely

*Yet I am not alone because the Father is with me.
I have said this to you, so that in me you may have peace.*
JOHN 16:32–33 NRSV

Maybe life gets busy, we move to a new city, or friendships may not be as easy to find as they used to be. We can find ourselves alone for a vast majority of reasons, some much harder than others. Being alone for long periods of time is hard and it comes with a lot of emotions. It's okay, it's completely normal to miss good things. You are likeable, you are loveable. Thankfully, and a bit ironically, there are quite a few of us who feel this way. Human connection is important, and craving good relationships and love is honestly not a bad place to start.

UNDERSTANDING THE WAY YOU CONNECT

Sometimes knowing what kind of connection we miss can help direct us in a way to finding something similar again. Loneliness is different for each person, as each person's community and closeness with others looks different.

In what ways do you feel companionship or closeness with people?

What are you missing the most about being around someone?

What does a good friendship look like to you?

FIND STORIES THAT RESONATE WITH YOU

Finding connection can also look like finding communities. Maybe it's people who share the same belief as you or who have similar interests.

Are there any communities you might be interested in joining?

Are there groups for things you do alone currently?

TRY REPETITION

Sharing space can be a good way of finding some new friends. Try showing up in the same place a few times a week. This could be a small community group, a gym class, an online group or club. Take note of the people you see often. Be brave and try striking up a conversation with one of them after a few times!

Where are some places you could go to meet people?

Write out a couple of good go-to questions to help spark some conversation between the two of you.

VOLUNTEERING

Volunteering can be another good way of making connections within your community. Maybe you could volunteer for a specific interest of yours? If you're a nature lover, perhaps you would have fun helping with something outside, or maybe you'd prefer a fundraising event?

What are some volunteer opportunities you might be interested in?

MAKING ALONE TIME MEANINGFUL

Let's try rephrasing loneliness to "alone time." What if you spent your time alone with intentionality? Learning, creating, or working on yourself can be just as important as our connection with others. While alone time may not be ideal at the moment, it might be just a bit better if we filled it with meaning.

How can you fill your "alone time" with meaning?

_____
_____
_____
_____
_____
_____
_____
_____
_____
_____
_____
_____
_____
_____
_____
_____

When You Don't Feel Like Cooking

*Listen! I am standing at the door, knocking;
if you hear My voice and open the door,
I will come in to you and eat with you, and you with Me.*

REVELATION 3:20 NRSV

This is a chapter for people who have recently felt uninspired with dinner. Balancing work, home life, and cooking can be a big endeavor. Some days you don't have time to cook; other days you may not even know what or how to cook. It's a shame that food doesn't buy and cook itself, right? It'd be so much easier. So, how do we re-find inspiration for dinnertime?

GIVING THANKS

Gratitude can help us feel more connected with the world around us. We'd like to take a minute and give thanks for the food that's been nourishing our bodies over the years. We're grateful for how it's helped us grow. We're grateful for the people who helped produce it. We're thankful to God who designed it.

What fed you recently?

How can you be thankful for it?

MEALS AND MEMORIES

What are your favorite memories that included food? What made these moments special? Maybe if we revisit some moments you really enjoyed, you might feel more like making something! Draw or write them in the space below.

COOKIN' WITH COLOR

Let's try to make a dish around a favorite color of yours. You might have to do some research on how to prepare new things you haven't cooked before. Make plans and record what you make below!

What's your favorite color?

_____
_____

What's the name of your dish?

_____
_____

What are the ingredients?

_____
_____
_____

HOW TO MAKE _____:

_____
_____
_____
_____
_____
_____
_____
_____

SPICE IT UP

What are some of your favorite spices? Maybe you like dill, chives, parsley, and paprika, or maybe you're a basil, chili, garlic, and olive oil kind of person. Take note of how often you use your go-to spices. Maybe it's time to try branching out? Try something new!

What are your go-to spices now?
_____
_____
_____
_____

What spices in your cabinet have you not touched in a while?
_____
_____
_____
_____

Is there something new you want to try cooking with?
_____
_____
_____
_____

MAKE IT THEMED

Think of one of your favorite movies with food in it. What sort of dishes are in the movie? What if you tried to recreate them? What could you decorate your dinner table with?

Write your answers here:

Think of some places you've traveled to or would love to travel to. What was the food you ate and loved, or what would you like to try? Could you recreate it in your kitchen?

Write your answers here:

ASK FOR RECIPES

Maybe there's some secret family recipe you've never tried, or your coworker always talks about this yummy-sounding salmon dish. Ask your family and friend groups for recipes they recommend. See what you can find. In the space below, write down the names of some people you'd like to ask:

NAME	YUMMY DISH

MAKE-IN-MIND

Think of someone you really appreciate. It could be a friend, a family member, or even someone you don't know personally. Try to make a dish dedicated to them. Maybe it's sweet with a hint of spice or it includes their favorite flavors.

Document it here:

Save This One For a Bad Day

*Call on Me in the day of trouble;
I will deliver you, and you shall glorify Me.*
PSALM 50:15 NRSV

Hey there. Sorry things haven't gone well lately. It's a pretty great thing you've picked up this journal though. Thanks for turning the pages that got you to this chapter. We're going to try to not focus on bad junk right now, as it's been a little too predominant lately. Let's take a minute and metaphorically escort what's making us feel so cruddy into its bed. We'll let it rest for now. Maybe we'll come back to it once we feel a bit more able to deal with it. But for now, it's time to decompress, relax, and remind ourselves that everything will be all right.

DEEP BREATHS

Picture yourself on top of a mountain. As you close your eyes, you can feel the chilly breeze against your skin and hear the ambient sound of wind gently dancing across the land around you. You take a deep breath in, hold it, and release. You can feel your shoulders relax, as the atmosphere seeps in and somehow helps things feel a little bit better. Maybe it's not a mountain, but perhaps there's a memory or place that helps you feel relaxed like this. If you can, try to picture yourself there. Take a couple deep breaths. Drink in the details. Does the air have a taste? Is the sun shining on your back?

Write what you find relaxing about your place below.

_____
_____
_____
_____
_____
_____
_____
_____
_____
_____
_____
_____
_____
_____

I SPY . . .

What's something in the room you're in right now that could help you feel a little better? Perhaps it's a pet or maybe an empty mug that has the potential of holding a warm drink. Draw or describe what you find in the space below.

DISRUPT THE FUNK

When we have a bad day, sometimes it helps to do something out of the ordinary. It can sometimes help reset things a bit. Maybe for you it means painting something, watching a funny movie to help boost your mood, or making a gift for someone you appreciate.

What are some other ideas for how you can help throw off the funk?

A GRAND ADVENTURE AWAITS

Let's pretend your bad day is a fantasy story. How could you picture the bad situations in a lighthearted, creative way? Maybe you're dealing with a scary sea creature or a deep, dark cave that's shrouded in mystery. Let's not get too ahead of ourselves, though. Let's start with the basics. Design your main character below.

Draw them here:

What is their purpose? Why are they drawn to adventure?

_____
_____
_____

What do they look like?

_____
_____
_____

What are their best qualities?

_____
_____
_____

Who, if anyone, will accompany the main character on this journey?

_____
_____
_____

THE HERO'S QUARREL

And so, with that, your character sets off toward their big adventure! Along the way they are met with some challenging news—tales of their most troubling foe yet. Your character decides to take time to carefully study their enemy. Knowing what they're up against will help them conquer them after all! (Pretend the bad situations in your life are a monster or villain. Let's describe them below.)

What does your villain look like?

_____
_____
_____

Draw them here:

What is their motive?

_____
_____
_____

What sort of things are they weak against?

_____
_____
_____

What hurts the main character the most about this enemy?

_____
_____
_____
_____

HOPE AWAKENS

Our hero readies for battle. The foe is strong, however, and leaves our hero and their allies hurt and stumbling for strength. It is in this moment that something truly miraculous happens. A glimpse of hope, a shimmer of light! An item floats from the sky, displaying the most beautiful reminders of why this battle is worth fighting.

What does this item look like for our hero?

What reminders does our hero see?

A DAY WELL SPENT!

A surge of strength pushes through the muscles of our hero's body, and they leap into action! With a single sweep of their mighty weapon, the enemy is badly wounded. It scurries away, for now. As our hero catches their breath, they realize the war is not over, but a battle well fought has ended. They pridefully return home, for today carried meaning and purpose: our hero has grown stronger, braver, and more courageous to fight another day.

Draw your hero's homecoming.

Growing Pains

*I am about to do a new thing;
now it springs forth, do you not perceive it?
I will make a way in the wilderness
and rivers in the desert.*

ISAIAH 43:19 NRSV

When we're young we learn that change is inevitable. Maybe we see our town change, friends move away, or we start to feel our bodies get older. Change can happen often in our lives. We may move states, leave jobs, or take root in unfamiliar communities. Our emotional states can change as well. We might outgrow our favorite hobbies, or we start to see the world around us differently. Adjustment is no easy feat. This chapter is here to help you explore some of the emotions that come with change, along with a few creative ways to approach the growing pains.

LET'S START WITH THE BASICS:

What's changing in your life right now?

Is there anything you've had to leave behind?

Is there something you're hoping for during this time of change?

SAILING YOUR BOAT IN UNPREDICTIABLE WEATHER

Try to imagine yourself as a sailor out at sea. As you navigate the world, you know you will come across some storms, but you're unsure how big the waves or how hard the sailing might be. You do, however, have the knowledge of your equipment and a crew of faithful members who are ready to help.

Color in the boat below!

SUPPLY SHOP

As you think about this time of change in your life, what kind of equipment or tools might look helpful to you? For a sailor and their storm, it's probably something that could help steer and direct the boat in bumpy waters. For your own journey, maybe it's listing out the consistencies in your life, scheduling in some relaxation time, or finding something to look forward to.

Let's brainstorm some options below.

YER TRUSTY CREW

Is there anyone in your life you can rely on when stuff gets a little crazy? Maybe a good friend or a family member? These people are part of your ship's crew. As captain of your ship, you'll need some right-hand people to help navigate and rig sails when storms come your way. Let's make a small log for the important roles on your ship. Write in the names and draw or paste pictures below.

CAPTAIN (YOU)

Name: _____
Picture:

1ST MATE

Name: _____
Picture:

2ND MATE

Name: _____
Picture:

3RD MATE

Name: _____
Picture:

MEMORIES AND MERMAIDS

If a sailor ever came across a mermaid out at sea, they'd probably keep that memory with them forever. They'd pass along the story to their crew, and maybe even try to paint pictures of what they saw. Maybe we could compare mermaids to some of our most beautiful memories? The really nice, rare moments. Over the miles of sea we cross and the storms we endure, we have these memories that keep the entire journey worthwhile.

Write some of these memories down below

Miracle

*Miracle [mir-uh-kuhl]: noun
- *an effect or extraordinary event in the physical world that surpasses all known human or natural powers and is ascribed to a supernatural cause.*
- *such an effect or event manifesting or considered as a work of God.*
- *a wonder; marvel.*
- *a wonderful or surpassing example of some quality.*

In the first book of the Bible, the author tells us that when God created everything, He said it was good. And when He created humans, He said they were *very* good.

As humans, we think thoughts and speak in languages others understand. We feel emotions. We make choices. We have the capacity to handle immense pain and sorrow.

And we *love*.

The fact that we are on *this* planet in the great expanse of the universe, at *this* time in the many years that have been and will be, with *this* life that we have, it's all an amazing, wondrous marvel.

We are a miracle for simply existing. And we are *very* good.

*(definitions from dictionary.com)

MIRACLE AFFIRMATION

Sit very still for just a moment and think, "I. am. a. miracle."
Did your shoulders tighten? Or relax? Are you clenching your jaw? Or smiling a bit? There's no right or wrong. Simply notice.

*Write out what comes to mind
when reflecting on that affirmation.*

OUR STAR, THE SUN

Draw as many stars as you can possibly fit on this page. Come back later and draw some more.

We would never, in our entire lifetime, be able to draw as many stars as there are in our universe. Out of all the stars in the galaxy, our planet circles one: our sun. And the earth is perfectly positioned away from the sun. It's not too close, where we would all burn up, and not too far, where we would all freeze to death. It's just the right distance to allow *life*.

Another amazing, wondrous marvel.

MIRACULOUS MOMENTS

We witness and experience the absolute miracle of life when we look at a newborn baby: their tiny toes and little nose, the way they let you know (loudly!) if something is bothering them, their instinctual nuzzle for their mother. As we get older, we tend to forget about our miraculous beginnings, or perhaps we don't quite believe ourselves to be that miraculous anymore. We're just ordinary citizens going about our ordinary lives.

It's good for us to look back and remember those moments in our lives—those newborn baby, miraculous moments. Such as when we met our person seemingly by happenstance, the way our hand can lift a cup of coffee to our lips, the idea of coming home to a place whose structure took centuries of engineering advances to create. When we get a glimpse of the divine right here in the midst of our ordinary, we can remember the amazing, wondrous marvel that we are.

Record some of your miraculous moments here.

_____
_____
_____
_____
_____
_____
_____
_____
_____
_____
_____

Record some more of your miraculous moments here.

STARGAZING

Sometime soon, pick a night when the skies are clear and look up at the stars. Marvel at the universe. If stargazing where you live is not possible for you, watch a video about the galaxy. Take a moment to remember just how big the universe is. Our galaxy is currently estimated to have more than 400 billion stars. And in the observable universe, there are probably more than 170 billion galaxies. And in that vast expanse, here you are. Living, breathing, loving, being. What. a. miracle.

MORE ABOUT THE STRUGGLE BUS

The Struggle Bus exists to help connect people and to remind us that it's okay to not be okay. It's okay to seek out the help you need. It's okay to feel alllll the feelings. It's okay to doubt and laugh and fail and burn out. Life is hard—but it is also good. We all find ourselves on *The Struggle Bus* at some point. We get on and off and back on again. What helps is having tools to get us through those hard times and to remember that we are not alone.

AVAILABLE SUMMER 2022

To learn more about
The Struggle Bus *collection,*
go to dayspring.com/the-struggle-bus.

MEET THE AUTHORS

AMBER

KATIE

Amber Maine and Katie Matzenbacher, friends and coworkers at DaySpring, learned they had a shared dedication for advocating for mental health. They continue to benefit from their own therapy and are passionate about sharing an empathetic approach to life's everyday struggles. Together they co-created *The Struggle Bus*, weaving their hearts, stories, and care into each new creation. *The Struggle Bus* collection has been a labor of love from the get-go, and they are so excited and thankful you are here.

It's Okay to Not be Okay was written by Katie and Amber, illustrated by Amber and designed by Jessica Wei. Special thanks to the team of people who helped bring this journal to you.

It's Okay to Not Be Okay:
An Interactive Journal to Help You Navigate the Hard Days
© 2022 DaySpring Cards, Inc. All rights reserved.
First Edition, March 2022

Published by:

21154 Highway 16 East
Siloam Springs, AR 72761
dayspring.com

All rights reserved. *It's Okay to Not Be Okay: An Interactive Journal to Help You Navigate the Hard Days* is under copyright protection. No part of this journal may be used or reproduced in any manner whatsoever without written permission except in the case of brief quotations embodied in critical articles and reviews.

Scripture quotations marked NIV are taken from THE HOLY BIBLE, NEW INTERNATIONAL VERSION®, NIV® Copyright © 1973, 1978, 1984, 2011 by Biblica, Inc.® Used by permission. All rights reserved worldwide.

Scripture quotations marked ESV are taken from the ESV Bible® (The Holy Bible, English Standard Version®) copyright ©2001 by Crossway Bibles, a publishing ministry of Good News Publishers. Used by permission. All rights reserved.

Scripture quotations marked NLT are taken from the Holy Bible, New Living Translation, copyright © 1996, 2004, 2007 by Tyndale House Foundation. Used by permission of Tyndale House Publishers, Inc., Carol Stream, Illinois 60188. All rights reserved.

Scripture quotations marked NRSV are taken from the New Revised Standard Version of the Bible, © 1989. Division of Christian Education, National Council of Churches. Used by permission of Zondervan Publishing House, Licensee.

Written by: Katie Matzenbacher and Amber Maine
Illustrations by: Amber Maine

Printed in Vietnam
Prime: J7485
ISBN: 978-1-64870-425-3